MW01170078

PRACTICE READERS
VOLUME 1: UNITS 1 & 2

PEARSON

Glenview, Illinois • Boston, Massachusetts • Chandler, Arizona • Hoboken, New Jersey

ISBN-13: 978-0-328-79572-7
ISBN-10:   0-328-79572-0
5 6 7 8 9 10 VOB4 18 17 16 15

Table of Contents

Dorothea Dix: Teacher and Reformer

by Natalie Caspari

Inflectional Endings -ed, -ing

accepting	improved	started
admired	included	suffering
allowed	leading	taking
allowing	learned	talking
cared	learning	teaching
caring	liked	training
caused	living	traveled
changed	looking	treated
continued	organizing	trying
ended	requiring	volunteered
explaining	returned	wanted
finding	shared	worked
helping	shocked	

Dorothea Dix was a teacher and a reformer. She cared deeply about problems that caused others to suffer. She wanted to help people have a better life.

In 1816 at the age of fourteen, Dix became a teacher. At nineteen she started her own school for girls in Boston, and she taught there for more than ten years. She then traveled to England. There she learned about the work of Florence Nightingale. Nightingale was a young nurse who had become famous for her work taking care of soldiers during a war. Dix admired Nightingale very much and wanted to be like her.

When she returned to the United States, Dix began teaching at a prison in Massachusetts. What she saw there shocked her. The prisoners were often treated very badly. Sometimes they were living without enough food, blankets, and clothes. At the time, people with mental illness were often put in prison even though they had done nothing wrong. They were treated even worse than other people in the prisons.

Dix began learning about this problem and trying to bring about changes. In 1843 Dix shared her information with the Massachusetts government, leading to important changes in the care of people with mental illness. Then she continued her work in other states, helping to start more than thirty hospitals. She also wrote a book explaining some of her ideas.

When the American Civil War began in 1861, Dix volunteered to work for the U.S. Army, organizing nurses to help take care of soldiers. At the time, women were not allowed in the army, not even in the hospitals. But Dix knew that women nurses could be brave and take good care of the soldiers. She worked hard to make the program successful. She made very strict rules for the nurses. These included allowing only women over thirty years old to join and requiring them to wear simple uniforms.

Eventually, more than 3,000 women worked as nurses. Dix worked with the army for five years, finding and training nurses, caring for soldiers herself, and looking for supplies for the hospitals. She was not always very well liked because of her strong opinions, but she greatly improved the way army hospitals were run, never accepting any pay for her work.

When the war ended in 1865, Dix continued helping people who were suffering, even though she was often sick herself. She even traveled to other countries, talking with the leaders about changes they could make to help people with mental illness. Like her hero Florence Nightingale, Dorothea Dix made a difference in the lives of many people. She changed the world with her courage and compassion.

The Wall Came Tumbling Down

by Mark Chen

Inflectional Endings -*ed*, -*ing*

allowed	died	reuniting
being	divided	risked
carried	escaping	standing
causing	guarded	stretching
celebrated	happening	topped
changed	including	tried
controlled	lived	trying
designed	offered	tumbling
demolished	planning	willing

For almost thirty years, the city of Berlin in Germany was divided by a huge barrier. A communist government controlled the eastern part of Germany, including part of Berlin, and the people there did not have much freedom. The other part of the city was controlled by a government that offered people more freedom.

The East Germans built a wall to separate the two parts of the city. The wall was designed to keep people who lived in East Berlin from escaping to the West. Many people tried to get past the Berlin Wall in hopes of reuniting with their family and friends. They risked their lives trying to escape to freedom.

The Berlin Wall was built of concrete, standing almost fifteen feet high and stretching twenty-eight miles through the city. It was topped with barbed wire, and soldiers guarded it carefully. Almost 200 people died trying to cross the wall. This structure was a symbol of sadness and fear for many people in Germany.

By the end of the 1980s, though, changes were happening all over Europe. The government in East Germany changed, now the leaders were more willing to let people travel to the West. On November 9, 1989, for the first time in almost three decades, the government allowed the people to cross freely into West Berlin. That same night many people came to the wall and celebrated. They carried hammers, picks, and other tools, planning to break the wall down. Before the day was over, they had demolished many parts of the wall, causing great joy in Berlin and around the world.

Why the Sun and Moon Live in the Sky: An African Folktale

Retold by Emily Beno

Inflectional Endings -ed, -ing

agreed	having	stayed
asked	liked	visited
bringing	noticed	visiting
building	reached	waiting
coming	rushed	wanted
crowded	sloshed	worried
finished	started	

The Sun and the Water were good friends. Sun often visited his friend, but Water never came to stay with Sun. One day Sun noticed this and wanted to make a change.

"Water, my friend, we should take turns visiting one another," Sun said. "It is not right that I am always coming as your guest, but you never come to see me."

Water agreed, but he was worried.

"I have a very large family," he said to Sun. "If I come with all of my family, your house will be very crowded. You must build a much bigger house so we can take turns visiting one another."

Sun thought this was a very good idea, so he rushed home to tell his wife, the Moon. She liked the idea of having a nice big house for visitors. Sun and Moon began building a bigger house right away. When they finished, they asked Water to visit.

Water came with all his family, and they started to fill the big house. The water soon reached as high as a grown-up's chest. "Is there still room?" Water asked.

"Yes, yes," said Sun, so Water kept bringing his family in. The water reached the ceiling, and Sun and Moon had to stand on the roof of the house.

"Is there still room?" Water asked. "My family is very large, and some are still waiting to come in."

"Yes, yes," said Sun, and soon the water was so high that it sloshed up over the roof. Sun and Moon had to go all the way to the sky, where they stayed ever after.

Space Exploration

by Trent Parelli

-er and -est

earlier	greater	quietest
earliest	larger	smaller
faster	loudest	strangest

In 1926 Robert Goddard, an American scientist, launched the first liquid propelled rocket. This rocket helped set the stage for the Space Age. But interest in space exploration began centuries earlier. In the 1600s Johannes Keppler, a German scientist, explained how objects orbit in space. In the 1700s creative writers described some of the strangest, most fanciful ships for traveling beyond Earth.

Robert Goddard invented and launched liquid-propelled rockets.

On October 4, 1957, space exploration became a reality. That's when the Soviet Union launched an artificial satellite, slightly smaller than a large beach ball, into space. A month later, the Soviets launched an even larger spacecraft, *Sputnik II*. The Space Age had begun. So too did the space race between the Soviet Union and the United States. These two countries competed to see which would have greater success in space exploration. Both countries sent up space probes (unmanned vehicles) and space vehicles carrying people.

The United States set a goal of landing people on the moon. On December 21, 1968, its *Apollo 8* became the first manned spacecraft to orbit the moon. This earliest moon orbiter set the stage for *Apollo 11*. In July 1969, with the words, "Houston, Tranquility Base here. The Eagle has landed," *Apollo 11* astronaut Neil Armstrong announced that Americans had achieved their goal. They had landed on the moon. A few hours later Armstrong became the first person to step foot on the moon's surface. Millions of television viewers around the world watched this history in the making on their televisions. One can imagine that the loudest cheers and quietest expressions of awe hailed this achievement.

Astronaut Buzz Aldrin was the second person to walk on the moon.

In the 1970s the United States began testing the space shuttle. The space shuttle was different from earlier space vehicles. What made it different was not its speed or its size. It was not faster or smaller than other space vehicles. It was different because it could be launched and returned to Earth over and over again. The space shuttle program ended in 2011, and three shuttles are now on display at Kennedy Space Center, the National Air and Space Museum, and the California Science Center.

The Space Age continues, however. Now nations that once competed in the space race cooperate to achieve success. Astronauts from nations around the world work together in the International Space Station orbiting Earth. Data from space probes provide more and more information about the universe.

The National Anthem

by Emily Falcone

-er and -est

earlier	higher	loudest
greatest	highest	prouder
happier	longest	quietest

The night of September 13, 1814, was not the quietest night at Fort McHenry in Maryland. At the time the Americans and the British were at war. A few weeks earlier the British had burned Washington, D.C. Now the British were attacking Fort McHenry near Baltimore.

Aboard a ship nearby stood American Francis Scott Key. He had come there to help free a doctor the British had captured in Washington. The British agreed to release the doctor, and Key could not be happier. But the British would not let them leave while the fort was under attack.

That night was one of the longest and loudest nights of Key's life. He was afraid that the light of day would show that the British had destroyed the fort. But dawn finally came, and as the sun rose higher, Key saw the American flag waving above the fort. Key surely had never been prouder or happier to see the flag. In his joy, he quickly wrote a poem once known as "The Defence of Fort M'Henry."

Later, the poem was set to the music of an old song, and it became known as "The Star-Spangled Banner." In 1931 the United States Congress adopted "The Star-Spangled Banner" as the national anthem. You can hear the anthem sung in schools, before sports events, and during official events. Although some people struggle to sing its highest notes, they always sing the anthem proudly. It remains one of the greatest symbols of the United States of America.

The New Pets

by Lisa Mendosa

-er and -est

bluer	cutest	quickest
bluest	largest	smaller
brightest	littlest	tiniest

When Dad asked what kind of pet Amy wanted, he was surprised by the answer. Amy didn't want a cat or a hamster. Amy wanted fish. At the pet shop, Amy and Dad looked at many colorful fish. The brightest and most colorful fish were swimming in the largest aquarium. Amy looked at them all including some with the bluest stripes she had ever seen. The stripes were even bluer than the sky. Amy's favorite fish, however, were tiny yellow fish with red spots. They were the cutest and quickest fish in the aquarium.

Today Amy's father buys her three of the littlest yellow fish. He also buys a small aquarium and some fish food. Dad lets Amy choose one of two small houses to put in the aquarium. Amy picks the smaller one as well as the tiniest pebbles and green plants for her aquarium. Amy and her father bring everything home. Amy holds a plastic sack filled with water and the three fish.

Amy puts the aquarium on top of the bookcase in her room. She puts the pebbles and plants in the aquarium. It looks like a garden. She makes a hill out of pebbles. Amy puts the stone house on the hill.

Finally Amy fills the aquarium with water. Then she gently puts her fish into the aquarium. She names the fish Fred, Ned, and Ted. Amy puts a pinch of food on the water and watches Fred, Ted, and Ned swim up to the food.

Solo Sailing

by Rebecca Janis

Suffix -or, -er

adventurer	owner	teachers
computers	sailor	teenager
diver	scanners	visitors
navigator	supporters	

Sixteen-year-old Laura Dekker was born to be a sailor. In fact, she was a sailor from Day 1. She was born on her parents' boat while they sailed near New Zealand! She lived on a boat for the first five years of her life, traveling with her parents. She loved being on boats, even as a very young child, and was the proud owner of a boat when she was just six. She began sailing solo soon after that. In 2010 this young adventurer from the Netherlands decided to take on her biggest challenge. She wanted to sail around the world. She would become the youngest person to ever do this solo, or alone.

Laura had some big hurdles to overcome first. Though her parents supported her, many people thought she was much too young for such a trip. They worried about her safety. They also worried that she would fall behind in school. Laura's family had to go to court to fight for her right to sail.

Laura was an excellent navigator, which means she could find her way using special tools and maps. However, she was required to carry special scanners, radios, and computers. These would help her plan her trip, stay on course, and stay in touch with her family. She had to learn advanced first aid in case she was hurt on the trip. According to the law, she also had to stay caught up with her schoolwork during the voyage. She did this by working with teachers through online courses.

Laura Dekker's Route

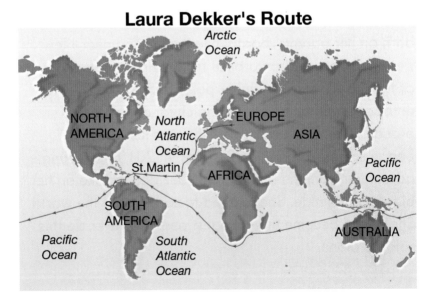

In August 2010 Laura set sail from the Netherlands in a small yacht she called *Guppy*. She sailed across the Atlantic, Pacific, and Indian Oceans. Then she came back across the Atlantic to the island of St. Martin. She finished her 27,000-mile journey at St. Martin on January 21, 2012. Her parents and younger sister, along with hundreds of supporters, were there to welcome her.

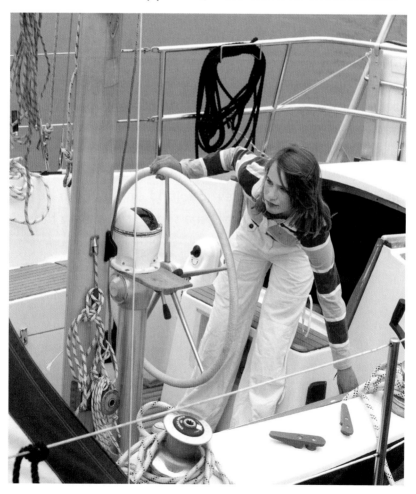

Laura had some big adventures and scary times during her 520-day trip. She stopped in many exciting and exotic ports. Her family met her at five of those stops. Other supporters came to cheer her on as well. In the Indian Ocean, she hid from pirates who were looking for her. They had heard about her journey on the news. She weathered bad storms and high winds that could have turned over her boat or swept her away. She even had some visitors in the open ocean. A whale came near the boat and soaked her with water, and flying fish landed right on her deck! Laura kept a very detailed journal about all that happened on her voyage. You can read it and see her videos and photos online.

Laura still loves to sail. She takes friends and family on trips with her now. She is also learning new skills. She decided to go back to New Zealand and learn to be a deep-sea diver. Obviously the sea keeps calling this teenager back to adventure and exploration.

The New Radio

by David Yeager

Suffix -or, -er

actors	cleaner	speaker
announcer	conductor	tuners
believer	performer	

Uncle Frank struggled as he carried a large object covered in an old blanket into the living room.

"What have you got there, Frank?" Grandma asked.

"You'll see," he said, winking at me. "Conrad, clear off that cabinet so I can set this down."

I leaped up and moved Grandma's workbasket from the table while Uncle Frank set the load down, took out his handkerchief, and wiped his forehead.

After we had all gathered around, Uncle Frank grandly pulled the blanket off like some performer doing a trick. We were all a little puzzled.

"What in the world is that?" Father asked.

"That," said Frank, "is a wireless."

"And what are we supposed to do with it?" Grandma asked.

"We listen to it," Uncle Frank said with a grin.

"Well, I've never heard of such a thing, sitting around listening to a box," Grandma said. "Of all the silly ideas, this has to be the silliest!"

Frank plugged the box in and began turning knobs, which he called tuners. After a few seconds of squeaking and squawking, we heard the voice of a speaker who was describing some kind of cleaner he had for sale. Then an announcer came on and introduced the program, which was a radio drama with different actors reading the parts of a very exciting story. Then there was music performed by a famous conductor and his orchestra. We listened all evening to the wonderful wireless. Even Grandma was a believer now, setting down her knitting to listen to the stories and music coming from our new radio.

Police Academy

by Alex Shull

Suffix -or, -er

drivers	leaders	protectors
helpers	learners	teachers
instructors	officers	trainers

Police officers have an important job as protectors and helpers. Just as people in other jobs do, police officers have to go to school to learn skills they need. That school is called the police academy.

At the police academy, people who want to be police officers take many different classes. They work with exercise trainers to get stronger and faster. They have to run, climb, crawl, and do lots of other exercises every day. They also learn to be very good drivers so that they can patrol the streets and respond quickly to calls. Driving instructors teach them how to drive in many different settings.

Teachers at the academy provide instruction in many different topics. Students learn about laws. They learn about the best ways to gather clues and evidence. They learn about psychology. That is the study of how people think and why they act the way they do. Students learn many ways to keep themselves and other people safe. They learn how to work well with other people. This includes other officers as well as all the people they are going to be helping. They also learn about being responsible leaders.

After students finish at the police academy, they take tests to make sure they are ready to be police officers. Then they begin to serve and protect their communities. But they are always learners. They continue to learn on the job even after leaving the academy.

Roller Coasters

by Matthew Gorman-Wright

Compound Words

brainstorm	landscape	uphill
downhill	seatbelt	waterfalls
framework	understand	

You climb into the seat, excitement building. You fasten the seatbelt. A worker pulls down the safety bar that will help hold you in place. Slowly, the car moves out of the station. Immediately it hooks onto a chain and begins the uphill climb to a peak overlooking the whole park. Then, with a rush, the car slips over the top. It races down the slope and around the track. It speeds through mind-boggling loops and turns. You hear the laughing and screaming of the other riders. It mixes with your own as the car zooms along the tracks. In a couple of minutes it's all over. You still feel the buzz of excitement. You can imagine the wind whipping your hair around. You can't wait to jump back in line. It's time for another ride on the roller coaster!

The first American roller coaster opened at Coney Island in Brooklyn, New York, in 1884. It only went about 6 miles per hour. Ever since then, thousands of roller coasters have been built around the country. The designers of these rides have made them taller, bigger, faster—all to bring more thrills for more people. Newer roller coasters can go more than 80 miles per hour! People continue to line up for the chance to feel the ultimate rush. Roller coasters are the most popular rides in most amusement parks today.

Roller coasters are amazing works of engineering and art. A roller coaster designer has to keep in mind lots of details when making a thrilling new ride. Safety is the most important part. Seatbelts and safety harnesses keep riders in the cars. Cars and tracks are made of strong materials. They need to handle the physical strain put on them. Designers have to make the framework strong enough. They have to make the hills, loops, and turns just the right size and shape to keep the cars moving right. This requires very good math and science skills. Designers have to understand gravity and other forces. They have to know how quickly a roller coaster will accelerate, or speed up, on a downhill portion so that they can build the tracks correctly. Though they try hard to make a roller coaster ride exciting, they make sure that the rides are as safe as possible before anyone rides them.

Of course, roller coaster designers also want to make rides that are interesting, exciting, and a little scary for all the thrill seekers. So they have to be creative. They might brainstorm together a long time to come up with good ideas.

Every amusement park is different. That creates another challenge for designers. They make roller coasters that fit the park. They think about size, theme, location, and landscape. The park owners may want the ride to go through waterfalls or a cave. They may ask for one loop or two loops. They may want a giant hill with a steep drop. Or they may want lots of gentle little hills so younger riders can enjoy it. Designers listen to these requests carefully. Then they use their imagination and special skills to come up with rides that thrill many riders every year.

Girl Scouts in the U.S.A.

by Amy Allison

Compound Words

artwork	birthplace	lifetime
basketball	campfire	sportswoman
birthday	headstand	

Juliette Gordon Low, nicknamed Daisy, was an active, artistic, energetic girl. As she was growing up, she loved to explore. The area around her birthplace in Savannah, Georgia, was a perfect place for her. She would run, swim, and go boating. She took care of her many pets, observed wild animals, and created all sorts of artwork. She was also a talented sportswoman. She learned tennis, basketball, rowing, and some gymnastics. Her special skill was standing on her head. Even as an adult, she still did a headstand to wish each of her nieces and nephews a happy birthday.

Low had a dream to make an organization where girls could learn to be active and involved. Her friend Agnes Baden-Powell had helped to start the Girl Scouts in Great Britain in 1910. She encouraged Low to do the same thing in the United States. On March 12, 1912, Low organized the first Girl Scout meeting in the United States, at her Savannah home. Eighteen girls came for this event. As the meetings continued, the girls played sports, learned camping skills such as pitching a tent and making a campfire, did service projects, and learned first aid. Other groups began to form too. Low continued to help the organization grow throughout her lifetime.

One century after that first meeting, there are now 3.2 million girls and women who are members of the Girl Scouts of America. More than 59 million women have been members over the years. Low's dream became a reality and continues to help other girls learn, grow, and reach their dreams too.

The U.S. Post Office Really Delivers

by Mina Markova

Practice Reader

Compound Words

airplanes	grandmother	postcard
faraway	mailbox	postmaster

Jacey is on vacation with her mom in Florida. After splashing around at the beach for a couple of hours, she sits down to write a postcard to her grandmother. She sticks a stamp on it and drops it in the post box. Three days later it arrives in her grandmother's mailbox in Oregon. How in the world did that card make it so far so fast? The U.S. Postal Service!

In 1775 Benjamin Franklin became the first postmaster of what would be the United States Postal Service. It was his job to organize ways for getting mail all over the colonies. Back then, it could take weeks for a letter to travel to a faraway city. Mail might travel by ship, by wagon, or by horse. For a short time in the 1860s the famous Pony Express was racing across the growing country.

Methods have improved since then. The use of airplanes and trucks has made delivery much faster. Now millions of pieces of mail cross the country and go around the world every day. Almost 160 billion pieces of mail were mailed in 2012. This included 70 billion first-class letters and postcards. More than 26,000 post offices handled this mail. More than 500,000 postal workers made it all possible. Think about that the next time you put a stamp on a postcard or check the mailbox at home!

The Fiesta

by Jeri Mahoney

Suffixes -ist, -ive, -ness

artist	expressive	native
brightness	festive	sleepiness
coolness	guitarist	tourist
creative	happiness	

Sara was too excited for words. This was her first visit to her grandparents' hometown in Mexico, just in time for a wonderful fiesta, or festival. When she awoke, the reminder of the fun day ahead drove all her sleepiness away. The beautiful native costume that grandmother had made for her lay across a chair. The bright colors and beautiful lace made her smile. Sara could picture herself dancing and twirling as the pink and yellow skirt swirled around her. She wasn't going to be just another tourist, either. Her grandfather, a guitarist, would lead a mariachi band in the parade. Sara was going to walk with him.

Already, even early in the morning, the whole town was colorful and festive. The brightness of the decorations, the smells of special foods baking, and the sound of mariachi bands warming up to perform added to the sense of excitement. The town square was filled with booths and people. Every window and doorway was decorated with flowers.

On this fiesta day, people celebrated the planting season. They hoped for their farms to have a good year. Everywhere she looked there were flowers and fruits in baskets. Grandmother brought some tomato and pepper seeds as part of the celebration.

There were many special foods for fiesta days. Sara tasted fresh mango and pineapple. She had a meat and corn stew with soft, hot tortillas. As the day got hotter, she cooled off with some horchata, a creamy rice drink

with cinnamon. And, of course, Sara had some of the nutty, crispy cookies her grandmother had made for the occasion.

Around 2 P.M., the annual procession, or parade, was to begin. As Sara walked with Grandfather to where they would start, she saw many sights. An artist knelt on the ground in the square, creating a beautiful chalk painting on the bricks. A creative puppet maker displayed his giant papier-mâché works of art. Women in dresses even more beautiful than her own dashed through the crowd to find friends. Sara hardly knew where to look. There was so much to see and do!

Soon, though, her attention was all on her grandfather. She had heard his band as they practiced, but she had never seen them perform like this. Their black pants and vests were trimmed in gold ribbon. Their broad hats were made of straw, and they wore bandanas of bright red silk around their necks. Their guitars were carved and painted with lovely designs. But best of all was the music. It was so expressive and exciting. It reminded Sara of all the happy times she had during her visit. She danced along beside the band as it entertained the crowds. Some people thought Sara was part of the act!

Finally, the procession ended. Sara wandered with her grandparents among the booths on the square. As the coolness of evening set in, Grandmother wrapped Sara in her beautiful shawl, and they walked slowly home together. Though she was tired, it was a long time before Sara could finally go to sleep. When she did, she dreamed of the happiness of the fiesta day and enjoyed it all over again.

Aunt Lisa's Mosaic

by Bea Clausen

Suffixes _-ist, -ive, -ness_

artist	happiness	perfectionist
cooperative	massive	quietness
creative	Native	

Adam had watched his Aunt Lisa making her artwork his whole life. She made mosaics, or pictures and designs formed from colorful pieces of stone and glass. Adam wanted to be an artist, too, but Aunt Lisa's mosaics were so creative and complex. It looked way too hard.

One day, Aunt Lisa came in very excited. "Guess what!" she said. "I've been asked by the community leaders to make a mosaic for the new park!" This was a real honor, because it meant her mosaic would be where hundreds of people would see it.

Aunt Lisa got to work on the design for the wall-sized mosaic right away. It would be massive compared to the other mosaics she had made. When the design was finished, and she was ready to begin creating the mosaic, she asked Adam to be her assistant.

37

Aunt Lisa was a perfectionist; she looked for stones that were just the right shape, size and color to fit the design. Together Aunt Lisa and Adam spent hours every day selecting and arranging stones and cementing them in place. Adam had a lot to learn, but Aunt Lisa was very patient. They liked best to work in the quietness of the early morning, before too many people were around. Slowly, the design took shape, showing pictures from the history of the town, with its Native American roots and pioneer past.

When the day finally came for the park to be opened and the mosaic to be unveiled, Adam got the surprise of his life. On a little plaque near the mosaic, he read:

"This mosaic is a cooperative effort of local artists Lisa Coburn and Adam Becker."

Adam grinned in happiness, because now he was an artist too!

Fireworks!

by Tyler Downs

Suffixes -ist, -ive, -ness

artist	chemist	extensive
awareness	darkness	festive
brightness	explosive	impressive
carefulness		

The night is quiet. The stars are beginning to peek out. You lay on the blanket looking up, wondering when the show will begin. Suddenly the darkness of the sky is lit up by a brilliant, colorful brightness. An explosive boom echoes from across the field. The fireworks show has begun!

Fireworks are a lot of fun to watch, but some people think they are even more fun to create. Pyrotechnicians are the people who create fireworks and set them up for displays. They are part chemist and part artist. As chemists, they have to learn how to put together the materials and set up the fireworks in a way that will be safe. As artists, they try to think of ways to make these wonderful light shows most impressive. They use chemicals and materials to create different colors, shapes, and effects. For example, some fireworks seem to glitter. Some have special shapes. Some seem to change colors. Pyrotechnicians have to have an awareness of fire safety. They have to know about weather conditions. They have to set up so the audience will be safe. It takes a lot of carefulness and attention to make sure no one gets hurt.

Depending on how extensive the show is, one show might use hundreds or thousands of fireworks. A whole team of pyrotechnicians will work together to make sure everything goes well. The result is a festive show of light and sound that takes the audience's breath away.

Fire Safety First!

by Charity Richards

Synonyms and Antonyms

broken, damaged/ functioning

calm (down)/ panic

careful, cautious/ careless

complicated/ simple

cool/warm, hot

danger/safety

dangerous, unsafe/safe

dark/light

firm, secure/ unsteady

forget/remember

frequently/ occasionally

high/low

new/old

When it comes to fire safety, you can never be too careful. Every year fire departments in the United States respond to more than a million fires. Many homes are damaged or destroyed each year. Hundreds of people die in home fires. Fires are dangerous and scary. That is why it is so important to learn how to keep you and your family safe in the event of a fire.

Fire safety doesn't have to be complicated. You can take a few simple steps to help protect your home. For example, learn to be cautious, not careless, about where you leave your things. Clothes, towels, papers, and other things can catch fire easily. Don't put them on lamps or other electrical appliances that can get hot. Don't leave them near open flames, such as a fireplace or a gas stove. Also, never use matches or lighters by yourself. Always ask for an adult's help. If you see that tall candles are unsteady, move them to a firm place. Get someone to help you make them more secure. A candle should never be left burning if no one is in the room.

Electrical fires can be prevented by paying attention to cords, outlets, and appliances you use in your home. Make sure cords and appliances are functioning properly. Any broken items should be discarded properly. You should also check to make sure outlets are not overloaded. Having too many things plugged into one outlet can cause shorts in the electrical system, which can lead to fires. Remember to always turn off anything you are not using.

You can also take steps to improve your safety in other ways. Remind your parents to install smoke detectors in your home. Make sure old batteries in the detectors are replaced with new ones, so you can be certain they work. These detectors should be tested frequently, such as once a month. Ask your parents about keeping a fire extinguisher in the house, too. Make sure everyone knows how to use it. It is also important to plan escape routes inside your home. It is a good idea to have more than one plan. That way, if one route is unsafe, you have another one ready to use. Talk to your parents in advance about a safe place to meet once you are out of danger. Occasionally organize a fire drill so you and your family can stay familiar with the plans.

If you do find yourself in a dangerous fire situation, make sure you stay low as you escape. That is because smoke will rise and fill the high spaces in a room first. If you crawl, you may be able to stay below the level of the smoke. If possible, cover your mouth and nose with a wet towel to protect yourself from the smoke. Also, check any door before you open it to see if it is cool or warm. A warm or hot door probably means the fire is nearby. In that case you need to use your other route to get out. If you forget something in a burning room, do not go back for it! You and your family are way more important than any possession.

You might expect a fire to cause a lot of light, but really it can be very dark because of all of the smoke. Fires are also very loud, which makes it especially scary and hard to think fast. But don't panic! Having a plan ahead of time will help you calm down in the event of a fire. That way you can think clearly to keep yourself and your family safe.

The Buzz About Honey

by Yvonne Lu

Synonyms and Antonyms

ancient/modern	dark/pale	light/rich, strong
bad/good	darker/paler	milder/stronger
bitter/sweet	ease, help	remarkable, wonderful

All day long, bees buzz from flower to flower. They are collecting nectar to carry back to the hive. There, worker bees transform it into a thick, sweet, golden liquid: honey.

45

Honey is a remarkable substance. It has been used for thousands of years by people all over the world. Of course you know that honey is used for sweetening. But perhaps you didn't know that it has other uses. Honey is a good natural antiseptic. That means it keeps bacteria from growing in a wound. People discovered they could put honey on cuts and burns to help them heal. Honey also is very good for keeping skin soft and hair shiny. People used it as a beauty treatment, in ancient times and in the modern day as well. Long ago it was also discovered that honey eases a bad cough. Now scientists have learned that this isn't just a folk tale. Honey really does help!

The color, taste, and smell of honey can vary. It depends on what kind of flowers the bees visited to gather nectar and pollen. For example, honey from acacia blossoms is paler and milder, while honey from avocado blossoms is darker and stronger. Basswood honey can taste a little bitter, though it is still sweet. A strong, dark honey makes the best "medicine." In fact, one company actually makes a skin medicine from manuka honey, which is a rich, dark honey. Typical "table honey"—honey used for everyday sweetening—tends to be pale golden and have a light flavor.

Whatever honey you use, and however you use it, remember what a wonderful discovery this sticky liquid is!

The Butterfly House

by Zach Washington

Synonyms and Antonyms

big, huge/little, small, tiny

bored/excited

bright, brilliant/pale

closed/opened

colorful/drab

delicate/rough

different, varied/same

first/last

new/old

"Wait for us!" Mom called after Kyra, but Kyra was just too excited to slow down. She had been waiting for the grand opening of the new Butterfly House at the zoo for weeks. She wanted to be among the first to go in.

Mom and her little brother, Kent, caught up to her at the gate. Kent looked bored, because he had wanted to see the giraffes first. But Mom had promised Kyra to go to the Butterfly House first, so they bought their tickets and went straight there.

They entered one set of doors and waited as the doors closed behind them. Then another set of doors opened to let them in. The old exhibit had just been in a small glass cage, but this new exhibit was huge. It contained a garden filled with the types of plants butterflies love. Visitors could walk along the stone paths to see the many butterflies.

The guide explained how no two butterflies are the same. The have different color patterns and varied wing shapes. Some are tiny and some are quite big. Some are brilliant, bright colors, while others are pale and drab. He also said the wings were very delicate. People who tried to catch the butterflies could damage them with a rough touch. Kyra was content to sit and watch, and even Kent seemed to enjoy the butterflies. Some came and landed on their heads and shoulders. Mom took a picture of the two children with their colorful friends. Kyra knew this would not be her last visit to this beautiful place.

Digging for Diamonds

by Jason Rhoades

The Uncle Sam Diamond was the largest diamond ever found in the United States.

Prefixes *un-* and *in-*

incapable	unaware	unlikely
incomprehensible	unbelievable	unplanned
incredible	uncomfortable	unpleasant
involuntary	unfamiliar	unwashed
unable	unhappy	

Jonas was uncomfortable and unhappy, sitting in the back seat of the car. It seemed they had been on the road for hours already, and the air conditioning hadn't been working. The unfamiliar landscape slipped by, but Jonas was unable to pay attention because of the heat.

"Crater of Diamonds State Park," his dad read from a road sign. "Says we can dig our own diamonds there." He glanced at Jonas in the rearview mirror. "Looks like you could use a break. What do you say?"

"I guess it could be cool," Jonas said with an involuntary shrug. They left the highway and followed the signs to a parking lot near the park's visitor center. Once inside, Jonas felt excitement rising. On the walls were pictures of some of the diamonds that had been found in the diamond fields there. Some had been found by people as they simply walked through the field. It was incomprehensible to Jonas that there would be diamonds just lying around for someone to find! Jonas thought it was unlikely he would find anything, but at least he would be able to say he'd hunted for diamonds.

One of the park rangers helped Jonas and his father get shovels and other tools to use and showed them the best way to search. He showed them pictures of what the unwashed diamonds looked like, so they would recognize one if they saw it in the dirt. Then he pointed the way to the fields, and they were on their own.

Jonas led the way to an area where there were no others digging. "Here goes," his father said before plunging a shovel deep into the black soil. He turned over a large clump of soil and broke it up. Then he and Jonas began sifting the soil just as the ranger had showed them. They picked through dirt, pebbles, and larger rocks. They were looking for the little glint that would tell them they had found a tiny treasure. The sun was hot and the digging work was dirty, but Jonas was incapable of staying grumpy. The thought of finding even one small diamond kept him going for more than an hour.

"We need to think about getting on the road again, son," Jonas's father finally said. Jonas was disappointed.

"One more shovelful?" he asked.

"Sure, one more," his father said. They dug in once more and began to sift. And there—in that last shovelful—Jonas saw what he'd been hoping for. He picked up the little stone and stared at it, unaware that his mouth was hanging open in surprise. The ranger looked over Jonas's shoulder and patted him on the back.

"You did it!" he said. "That's the first diamond anyone has found this month." The ranger led them back inside to measure and photograph the little brown diamond. Then he dropped it into a tiny plastic container and handed the container to Jonas. "You mean I get to keep it?" Jonas asked.

The ranger nodded and grinned. "Finders, keepers. That's our motto here." Jonas tucked the diamond safely into the pocket of his jeans and followed his father to the car. It was completely unbelievable that he had a diamond of his own in his pocket! That incredible find on that unplanned stop turned an unpleasant trip into the best road trip of Jonas's life.

The Longest Leap

by Carolina Turek

Prefixes *un-* and *in-*

incorrect	unbelievable	unhooked
incredible	unbroken	unknown
indefinitely	uncommon	unsafe
unable	unexpected	unusual
unafraid		

Skydiver Felix Baumgartner has done some unbelievable jumps in the 28 years that he has been diving. He has jumped from unusual and unexpected places all over the world. But on October 14, 2012, he did something truly incredible: he skydived from space. He set out to break a skydiving record for the highest jump that had been unbroken for 50 years.

Baumgartner had two balloons prepared to carry him into space, but he had unexpected problems with the first. That meant he had one chance left to complete the jump, or he would have to wait indefinitely for another chance. The balloon carried Baumgartner in a special pod almost 39 kilometers (more than 24 miles) above the earth's surface. He adjusted his special suit so that it would protect him in the thin, cold air. An incorrect move could have had dangerous results. He carefully opened the door and stepped onto the platform. Unafraid, he unhooked himself and then jumped into the unknown. No one knew what would happen to him as he sped toward the ground. Would he be able to control the fall safely? Would his body be able to handle the uncommon forces he would experience while falling so far and so fast?

Baumgartner was in freefall (meaning he didn't have his parachute open) for nearly five minutes. In that time, he sped up so much that he was going faster than the speed of sound. For a while he was unable to control his spinning. It was creating very unsafe pressure on his body. But soon he gained control, and he landed safely in the New Mexico desert. In those ten minutes, Felix Baumgartner had leaped out of space and into skydiving history.

The Welcome Party

by Lynette South

Prefixes *un-* and *in-*

inability	uncertain	unsafe
incomplete	unexpectedly	unsure
insecure	unknown	

We waited a little nervously at the airport. Mom stood beside Ms. Cofax, who held a sign with the name of the family we were there to meet. Ms. Cofax worked for an organization that helped refugees. Refugees are people who have to leave their home countries, often unexpectedly, because it is unsafe to stay anymore. Mom had signed us up for a program called First Friends to welcome a refugee family. We would help them get used to life in our city.

Ms. Cofax had explained that often refugees are afraid and uncertain when they arrive. Their inability to speak English well might make them feel insecure. They might be unsure of American customs. That was why it was so important for people like us to be their friends.

A crowd of people began to come through the doors. One family scanned the waiting area. A smile lit the woman's face when she saw our sign. She touched her son's shoulder and pointed in our direction. Ms. Cofax introduced us to this unknown family and asked them about their trip.

I could tell the boy was about my age. He was as shy and uncertain as I felt. But I wanted him to feel welcome. While the adults talked, I showed him some origami animals I had made. One was still incomplete, and we worked together to figure out the last folds. I found out that Wahid spoke English pretty well. We talked about school and after-school clubs. He wanted to know if there was a soccer team in my neighborhood and where he could go to bike. Before we left the airport, Wahid and I were already friends. I knew I'd have as much to learn from him as he would from me.

Chocolate

by Ben Kelp

> **Word Origins**
>
> | | | |
> |---|---|---|
> | benefits | chocolate | manufactured |
> | caramel | cinnamon | pretzels |
> | chili | colonizing | royalty |

Chocolate is probably one of the most popular foods of all time. How did this well-kept secret from Central America become so loved around the globe? It began as a bitter drink made from ground beans. It was transformed into a delicious tasty treat. It happened because of European dreams of colonizing the world.

The Aztecs and other Central American peoples used the dried beans of the cacao plant to make a hot drink. This drink was rich and flavorful, but not sweet like chocolate usually is today. A Spanish explorer named Hernan Cortes got a taste of the chocolate drink in 1519. He was visiting at the court of the Aztec king Montezuma II. Cortes was very impressed.

In 1528, Cortes returned home with a whole load of the beans. The Spanish added sugar and cinnamon to

Montezuma II was the king of the Aztec Empire when Hernan Cortes arrived in Central America.

the bitter drink. They kept this treat secret for about a century. But then the secret got out. Soon chocolate was enjoyed by royalty across Europe. Some places began to sell chocolate. It was so expensive, however, that only the wealthy could afford it. In the 1700s the prices fell. Chocolate became more widely available. It even became available in the American colonies. James Baker and John Hanan opened a cocoa mill in Massachusetts so the treat could be manufactured there.

Until 1828 chocolate could only be drunk. No one had figured out how to make it into a solid. After many experiments, a Dutch chemist named C. J. van Houten found a way to press the fat out of cacao beans. He separated the beans into cocoa powder and cocoa butter. Cocoa butter is the rich, creamy, light-colored fat. These parts could then be remixed in different amounts to make a paste. This was the first "eatable" chocolate.

Since then, many different varieties of chocolate have been produced. Milk or cream was added to make milk chocolate, a creamier, lighter version. White chocolate is made with cocoa butter but no cocoa powder. Chocolate is mixed or filled with other things to make combinations that might be delicious, unusual, or just plain odd. You can try chocolate with mint flavoring, nuts, caramel, fruit, marshmallows, pretzels, hot chili, even crispy bacon! Cocoa powder is also used to make chocolate baked treats. Some Mexican recipes still use unsweetened

A worker in a chocolate factory checks the chocolate being produced.

cocoa or bittersweet chocolate to season meats and sauces.

Chocolate isn't just a tasty treat, either. It seems to have some good health benefits, too. Chocolate contains a chemical that goes to the brain and helps improve a gloomy mood. Scientists have also found that an occasional bite of dark chocolate can help the heart. Cocoa contains something called flavanols. These chemicals can improve blood flow and lower blood pressure. Other studies found that another chemical in chocolate may help fight tooth decay. In fact, scientists want to add that chemical from chocolate to toothpastes and mouthwashes. All that doesn't mean you should run out and gobble down something chocolate. Remember: Chocolate contains lots of sugar and fat. These can quickly undo any good effects of eating chocolate. Darker chocolates have more benefits. Those with a cocoa content of more than 60 percent are healthiest. But moderation is very important. If you want to have chocolate, keep the amount small. Then enjoy every last bite!

Our Garage Band

by Rachel Cho

Word Origins

audiences	harmonica	quintet
banjo	jazz	ukulele
combination		

Luke had received a new drum set for his birthday. All he could think about was how great it would be to start a band with his friends. He could imagine audiences cheering wildly as he twirled his drumsticks and then counted off an awesome beat. He shared his idea at lunch the next day and asked his buddies to join him in his band.

Larissa said she was learning to play the ukulele. She was eager to give it a try in the band. Luke wasn't quite sure a ukulele would go with his drums, but he agreed she could come.

Daniel said proudly that he had learned to play the banjo, thanks to his Uncle Curt. A banjo has strings like a ukulele, he said, so they could probably play all right together.

Shawn pulled his new harmonica from his pocket and played them a little tune to show his skill. Kari patted the trumpet case beside her and said she would be happy to try. She had studied a lot about jazz musicians, and she thought she'd like to be one too. They agreed to meet for practice on Saturday. The whole quintet was together that afternoon.

They made some interesting music together. It wasn't quite rock or jazz or any other style of music they knew about. Luke thought it might have been the first-ever ukulele-trumpet combination in the history of music. They had fun together, but in the end they came to a decision. They would stop being a band and go back to being lunch buddies, which was just as fun, but no practice required!

Make Your Own Papier-Mâché Project

by Susan Scofield

Word Origins

balloon	methods	sculptures
furniture	papier-mâché	

Get paper wet and mix it with glue, and what will you have? It might sound like a big mess, but it can actually become a work of art. The material is called papier-mâché. For centuries, artists have used papier-mâché methods to make sculptures, furniture, boxes, toys, and masks. The paper and glue can be molded and dried to form almost any shape. These objects are painted and glazed, creating beautiful, colorful art. It's not as hard as you might think.

You can try papier-mâché at home. It is easiest to practice on a round balloon first. You can try other shapes later. You will need a balloon, newspapers or paper towels torn into short strips, flour, and water. You might also want to cover your work area with newspaper and put on some old clothes.

First, blow up the balloon. Then put some flour in a bowl. Add water very slowly, stirring to get rid of any lumps. Your mixture should be pretty thin when you are done. When you are ready, take a strip of paper and dip it in your flour paste. Let extra paste drip off, and then put the strip on the balloon and smooth it out. Keep doing this until you have a layer of paper strips all over the balloon. Leave this to dry completely, and then repeat. You can have as many layers as you want. Just make sure you let each layer dry before adding the next one. When you are done, you can paint the whole thing. Then hang it up where everyone can admire your very own papier-mâché work of art.

3, 2, 1, Blast Off!

by Liz Torres

Latin Prefixes *dis-, re-, non-*

disagreed	nonsense	repacked
disappeared	reappeared	replace
disliked	rearranged	reread
disorder	relaunch	reuse
nonflammable		

Today was the day. Jay and Glendy had been counting down to the launch of their uncle's new model rocket for over a month. As a member of the local rocket club, Uncle Scott had built and launched dozens of rockets. However, this one was different, because this time Glendy and Jay would be at his side for the whole thing, so they could see all the steps involved. They were junior members of the rocket club now, and this would be their first project.

When Scott came home with the kit, the three of them had rushed to open it and get a look. The basement, where Scott always worked on his rockets, was in complete disorder for two days. Parts of the rocket and pages of instructions were scattered everywhere. But soon they had rearranged everything and gotten the basement back in order.

Scott made them read and reread the instructions to make sure they followed each step perfectly. Every day after school, when homework was finished and chores were done, Jay and Glendy joined Scott in the basement to fit in a little more time with the rocket. Finally, Scott announced that it was ready to paint.

At first they disagreed about colors and trim. Jay thought it should be white or silver so it would look like a real rocket. Glendy thought that was too boring. She wanted it to be hot pink, so they would see it clearly as it lifted into the air, but Scott and Jay both disliked that idea. They settled on using mostly silver and red for the rocket and trim. Scott announced that the official launch would be the following Sunday.

The day was clear and the sun shone brightly. They drove out to the field where Uncle Scott always set up his launches. He had a nonflammable mat that he always used and a rod to hold the rocket upright. He gently set the rocket on the rod and prepared it for flight. He hooked up the control that would ignite the motor. "No nonsense now, kids," he said seriously to Glendy and Jay. "This is the moment of truth." They stood back and held their breath as Scott pushed the launch button. For a second nothing seemed to happen. Then, with a gentle roar, the rocket slowly lifted off and sped into the air. They watched it arch high above them and then fall back toward the ground. A little parachute popped out to carry the rocket gently back to earth. As they watched, the rocket and parachute disappeared into a cluster of trees.

Scott jogged off to find the rocket. He reappeared a minute later with the rocket in hand. They repacked the rocket and equipment in the car and drove home. "What did you think of that?" their uncle asked.

"That was so cool!" Glendy gushed. "I can't wait to make another one."

Jay shook his head. "I agree that it was cool, but can't we reuse this one? We spent a whole month making it. I'd like to get more than one launch out of it after all that work."

"Right you are, Jay," Scott said. "I'll replace the motor, and we'll relaunch this one next week, same time, same place. How's that sound?" The children cheered. They would see this rocket soar again.

Tall Tale or Truth?

by Kelley Baruch

Latin Prefixes *dis-*, *re-*, *non-*

disbelief	nonsense	replaced
dishonest	repay	return
dislodged		

Sam wasn't exactly dishonest, but sometimes his stories just sounded a little far-fetched. I never knew quite what to believe when he started telling a crazy tale.

"One day," he told me, "I was out walking in the hills yonder, and my boot dislodged a rock. As that little rock tumbled down, others started to slip after it, and soon I lost my footing and slid clear to the bottom. I dusted myself off, replaced my hat on my head, and then I saw it. Lying on top of the heap of rocks was the prettiest diamond ring you've ever seen. Well, I slipped it on my little finger, thinking what a lucky man I was, and went on my way. When I got to town, while I grabbed some dinner at the diner, the cook took one look at the diamond and whistled.

'That sure is pretty,' he said. 'Looks like something fit for a princess.'

No sooner had he said that than a lovely young woman came up to me. She was a princess for sure!

'Excuse me, sir,' she said. 'I couldn't help overhearing what that man said. I lost my ring, and I would be grateful to have it back. I would be happy to repay your kindness if you'd return it to me.'

I gave her the ring, she thanked me sweetly, and I left a happy man."

I stared hard at Sam when he finished his story. "That's all nonsense, Sam! How did you know she was a princess?" I asked in disbelief. "You just gave a diamond ring to a stranger?"

Sam unfolded the newspaper and showed me the front page. There was a picture of the little princess, a *real* princess, who was making a visit to the town. Even in black and white, the diamond seemed to sparkle on her hand.

Dogs Lend a Helping Paw

by Jillian Vaclaw

Latin Prefixes *dis-*, *re-*, *non-*

disabilities	disrespectful	reinforcement
disobey	nonstop	remove

Dogs can be good friends and helpers to people. However, guide dogs have a special job to do. They help people with disabilities, especially visual disabilities, to get around safely.

Guide dogs are trained from the time they are puppies to do their job. A good guide dog has to be smart, calm, and well-behaved. It has to learn not just to obey commands, but also to disobey unsafe commands. It cannot bark a lot or chase after squirrels and cats. These dogs go into buildings and restaurants and have to be around strangers a lot. So trainers teach them to be very polite and quiet. Guide dogs are trained using positive reinforcement. That means they are rewarded every time they do something correctly. That way, they remember the right thing to do and eagerly try to get it right every time.

These special helpers have a big job to do. They learn to guide their owners carefully. They stop when there is a step or curb. They watch for things that might cause harm, such as moving cars. They remove their owners from paths where something is in the way.

A guide dog is on duty nonstop when it is out with an owner. It can be disrespectful to pet or distract a guide dog while it is working. Always ask the owner first. These hardworking dogs deserve the love and respect their owners and anyone else give them.

Holding Back the River

by Rich Luttrell

Compound Words

anything	floodwaters	safeguarding
ballgame	hallway	sandbags
downpour	handshakes	sidewalks
downstairs	homework	something
downtown	newspaper	sunrise
everyone	raindrops	wheelbarrow
everything	rainstorms	without
firefighter	riverbank	workload
flashlights	riverside	workout

It seemed to Rob that it had been raining for days and days without end. Every bit of ground was a soggy, muddy mess. The sidewalks and streets had puddles that had grown into ponds. Every pair of shoes he owned was in a different state of dampness. Every ballgame had been canceled that week, and now they were talking about closing the school until the rainstorms were done. He wondered when there would finally be a break in the weather.

He had finished his homework but still sat at the table staring out the window at the endless downpour. He heard the front door open and close. The bustle in the hallway told him his dad was home and shedding his dripping rain gear before coming in.

Rob's father looked very serious when he finally walked into the living room. "They said on the radio the river is going to come out of its banks tonight," he said to everyone gathered there.

"But that will flood half the town!" Rob's mother said, shocked. "Isn't there anything they can do to stop it?"

"Well, they were asking for volunteers to help fill sandbags and build up a barrier," Dad said. "I thought I'd change into some old work clothes and go help out."

Rob felt a strong desire to help, too. His best friend Michael lived just a few blocks from the riverside. He hated the thought of Michael's neighborhood being flooded. "Would it be all right if I came with you?" Rob asked.

"I expect they will need all the help they can get to handle this workload," Dad said. "Go get changed while I grab some tools and flashlights, just in case."

They left a few minutes later and headed to the downtown garage where the work was being done. After a quick greeting, they were shown where to work and what to do, and they got right to work. There were a hundred people already there.

Side by side, Rob and his dad filled empty bags of rough fabric with sand and silt, then each bag was loaded into a wheelbarrow and wheeled down to the riverbank. When Rob looked in that direction, he was alarmed to see how high and fast the river was rising. It seemed impossible that they could stop all that water. Slowly, the wall of sandbags had taken shape and grown. As each section was finished, it was covered with a plastic sheet, which was secured with bricks and more sandbags. They worked until almost 11 P.M. to build a wall to stop the floodwaters.

"We've done everything we can do," said the firefighter who was overseeing the work. "Thanks for your help, everyone. We all hope this hard work will pay off in safeguarding our community." After a round of handshakes with their fellow volunteers, Rob and his dad went home, dripping, dirty, and hoping very much that the firefighter was correct.

Rob awoke at sunrise the next morning, his whole body aching from the long workout the night before. After a few minutes, he realized something was missing: the sound of raindrops on his window. The rain had finally stopped! He raced downstairs to see if there was any news. Dad smiled as he set down his newspaper. "The sandbags stopped the water," he said. "We helped save our town!"

Living Small

by Sherry Cain

Compound Words

anywhere	cupboards	highway
bathroom	downside	lifestyle
bedroom	everyone	nowhere

Bigger is better, right? Some people say that's not always the case when it comes to choosing a home. One of the latest trends in housing is what are called micro homes. People can buy or build these tiny houses to save space and money and to be kinder to the environment.

Micro homes are generally less than 500 square feet in size, and some are as small as 65 square feet, which is smaller than a small bedroom in most regular homes. Imagine fitting a whole house—bedroom, bathroom, kitchen, and all—into your bedroom! These houses usually have small-scale furniture and appliances made to fit. They also have clever design features—such as special cupboards and cabinets—that make living in such a small space more convenient. In addition, many of these homes are portable. They can be loaded onto a truck and carried down the highway to anywhere you want to go.

Many people truly love living in their tiny spaces. They say life is simpler, with less house cleaning, smaller bills, and fewer belongings to worry about. On the downside, though, there is nowhere for house guests to sit and visit. Nor can the owners store many things. They have to learn other ways to accomplish these goals. Not everyone is cut out for such a trimmed-down lifestyle. Families with children would probably find the small spaces hard to deal with. People who like to have parties would also have trouble.

Does the thought of living in a small space sound interesting to you? Perhaps when you are older, you'll be ready for a tiny micro home of your own.

Busy at the Quilting Bee

by Mindy Homme

Compound Words

bedspreads	faraway	patchwork
buttermilk	hardworking	something
daylong	henhouse	whatever
everyone	homesteads	

Out on the American Great Plains, homesteads were far apart and neighbors rarely saw each other. Pioneer women had plenty to keep them busy. There was a houseful of people to care for, and chickens to look after in the henhouse. There was bread to bake, buttermilk to churn into creamy butter, and clothes to wash and mend. There was a garden to tend and candles and soap to make. There was always something to do, but it was a very lonely life. It was this loneliness that led to one of the most social and joyful pioneer traditions. Quilting bees brought faraway friends and neighbors together.

Quilting is a very old craft. It has been done in many cultures around the world. Quilting is a way of putting together several layers of fabric, which create a soft, warm covering. It was used to make warm protective clothing. Later, more and more quilters made blankets and wall hangings.

Pioneer women often made patchwork quilts. They used scraps of whatever fabric they had to create colorful quilts. Quilts were valued not just as warm bedspreads. They also served as door, window, and floor coverings. However, hand stitching a quilt is time-consuming. These women solved that problem by having a daylong get-together to finish up a quilt. The men and children might come as well. Then everyone would have dinner together, followed by an evening of music and dancing. Quilting bees could turn into quite a party. They were a great treat in the lives of the hardworking pioneers.

Johnny Appleseed

by Tanya Cox

Suffix -ly

affectionately	happily	really
carefully	kindly	respectfully
contentedly	nearly	simply
eagerly	obviously	supposedly
extensively	oddly	usually
faithfully	politely	warmly
generously	rarely	wisely

The story of Johnny Appleseed is one of America's great legends. But Johnny Appleseed wasn't a legend at all. He really lived and really planted apple seeds. His real name was John Chapman. In 1792, at the age of eighteen, Chapman set off on his travels. His younger brother came with him for a while, but for most of his life, Chapman traveled alone. He was warmly welcomed wherever he went and had friends everywhere. The adults liked to hear whatever news he brought. The children listened eagerly to his stories. Even when someone would kindly invite him to stay, Chapman usually politely refused. He contentedly slept on the ground beside a small campfire. He seemed to prefer to stay close to the soil in which he planted his seeds.

Chapman's goal was to move into the West ahead of the settlers, sowing apple seeds all along the way so there would be food for all. John Chapman traveled extensively for nearly fifty years. He went to Pennsylvania, Ohio, and Indiana. He picked up seeds for free at apple cider mills, and he planted them wherever he thought they would grow well.

Later stories about Chapman, or Johnny Appleseed as he was affectionately called, made it sound as though he just threw seeds anywhere. However, Chapman usually put a lot of care and thought into his planting. He planted trees, sometimes whole groves of them, in places with healthy soil, enough water, and some kind of natural protection. He would carefully build fences around new trees to keep animals away. He would go back and check on the trees when he had a chance. He planted thousands of trees this way. He sold some of these trees to have money to live on. Others he traded for things he needed. Others he simply gave away.

Chapman dressed oddly and wore shabby clothes, but it wasn't because he was poor. It was because he would often generously give away his clothes. He rarely wore shoes, preferring instead to run around barefooted. Supposedly the skin on his feet was so tough that he could walk on ice and snow without feeling the cold. He wore funny homemade hats. Always, no matter what, he had his leather pouch filled with seeds slung over his shoulder.

Chapman was a friend to the Native Americans as well as to the settlers. He treated them respectfully and learned a little of their languages. He was able to speak at least basic words with several different tribes. He honored nature much in the same way as the Native Americans did. His diet consisted of the fruits, nuts, and berries he could find.

In 1842 Chapman stopped his wandering ways. He went to live with his brother in Ohio. Chapman took a final trip west in 1845. On that visit to Indiana, he got sick and died. Legend said that was the first (and obviously last) time Johnny Appleseed ever got sick.

Truth and fiction have gotten a little jumbled in the case of John Chapman. He became known as a larger-than-life character who happily cast apple seeds everywhere he went. In truth, he planted wisely and proved himself to be a good businessman. However, the legends are fun to hear. Therefore storytellers still faithfully tell the tale of the great and kind Johnny Appleseed.

Uncovering Fossil Finds

by Tom Follvik

Suffix -ly

carefully	gradually	roughly
carelessly	methodically	slowly
closely	patiently	thoroughly
eventually	perfectly	tirelessly
gently		

Dr. Zorn has worked patiently for weeks. She has run tests, studied photographs, and examined other findings from the area. Now it is time to get below the surface … and uncover a dinosaur!

Dr. Zorn is a paleontologist, or a scientist who looks for and studies fossils. Workers discovered a tusk at this site, and now it is her job to reveal the great beast it belonged to. Like every good fossil hunter, she works slowly and methodically to uncover fossils. At first she and her team used shovels and larger equipment. Now they are too close. Digging roughly or carelessly could damage the fragile fossil remains they are trying to preserve. Dr. Zorn spends hours on her hands and knees with a pick, gently chipping away little pieces of stone. Soon the work will be even more delicate, with a fine chisel and a small brush. The hard work pays off. As she tirelessly works, a magnificent skull is revealed. It is the head of a giant mammoth, almost perfectly intact.

Dr. Zorn and her team continue to gradually free the mammoth fossils from the stone. Eventually, they will carefully lift the skull out of the pit and into a crate. There it will be cushioned and protected for the trip back to the lab. Once there, she will be able to clean it more thoroughly and examine it more closely. Who knows what secrets this mammoth might be hiding about long-ago life on Earth?

Going for Gold

by John Marcotte

Suffix -*ly*

certainly	nicely	regularly
faithfully	properly	successfully
healthfully	really	usually

He has competed in four Olympic Games, successfully bringing home three medals. He has been one of the top-ranked martial artists in the world since he was a teenager. With that kind of experience, Steven Lopez knows what it takes to be a champion.

Lopez trains really hard all the time, working out two or three times every day. He does martial arts practice faithfully every morning. Then he does other exercises in the afternoons. He needs to be strong and fast to compete in his sport, tae kwon do. It helps that his brothers Jean and Mark and his sister Diana also train with him. They push each other to improve, and not always nicely! Mark and Diana have both competed at the Olympics too. Jean has been their coach.

Working out regularly is only part of the training. Lopez also has to eat healthfully. He uses up a lot of energy when he trains, and he pushes his muscles hard. He has to eat healthy foods that give him energy and heal his muscles. For example, on the day before a competition he usually eats chicken, rice, and vegetables. On the day of a competition, he prefers peanut butter sandwiches and fruit. These are light and give him quick energy.

Steven Lopez pushes himself hard. He also knows how to properly take care of his body. And he gets support and encouragement from his family. That certainly seems to be a recipe for success in sports and in every other part of his life.

Desert Dwellers

by Kim Duran

Unknown Words

astounding	desolate	irrigation
averages	ecosystem	nomads
continental	inhospitable	scarce

The Sahara covers an enormous stretch of northern Africa. It is among the largest deserts in the world. It covers an astounding 3.3 million square miles. That's bigger than the 48 states of the continental United States! Picture that: Every state from Maine to California covered in endless stretches of hot sand.

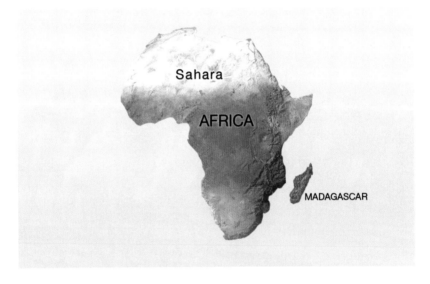

The Sahara averages only about three inches of rain each year. Mostly it supports only short grasses, small shrubs, and a few tough trees. Temperatures soar near 120 degrees Fahrenheit in the hot season. They can plunge to freezing at night. In spite of the harsh conditions, 2.5 million people live in the Sahara. Artifacts found in the desert show that even more people lived there in the ancient past. They may have lived around large lakes that have since disappeared.

People of the Sahara usually live in one of two ways. Many are nomads. They travel with livestock to wherever the grasses are. Mostly they raise sheep, goats, and camels. Some have cattle and horses as well. In times of drought, they may have to travel quite far to find pasture for their animals. Feeding a lot of animals on a small area of pasture leads to the problem of overgrazing. This can leave the land even more desolate. Nomadic herders sometimes clash with one another over the scarce resources.

These nomads were very important in African history. They kept trade routes open between North Africa and sub-Saharan Africa. They knew the routes and aided the traders in their journeys across the dangerous desert.

Other desert dwellers have settled down to raise crops. An oasis is an area of land in a desert where pools of water collect or where there is a larger supply of groundwater. The supply of water allows more plants to grow. The oasis dwellers often have gardens or small farms. Irrigation systems bring water to their crops. They grow grains, pumpkins, vegetables, and some fruit trees. The wells in these areas have to be guarded carefully. Blowing sand and shifting dunes can make them unusable. People spend a lot of time and energy cleaning and protecting their water. Even so, increasing water use around oases is threatening this lifestyle by causing water levels to drop.

A third group of desert dwellers has grown over the years. These are specialists, people with a skill that can help the farmers or the herders in their work or living. Blacksmiths, mechanics, weavers, water engineers, teachers, and doctors are part of this third group.

Communities of desert dwellers might have a little trading store where they can get basic goods, but they also rely upon "hawkers," who travel among these communities with goods they might want or need. The "hawkers" might have cloth, seeds, machine parts, or luxury foods to sell.

Drought and famine, dangerous sandstorms, and changes in the ecosystem of the desert are realities of life in the desert. They are driving many in the Sahara out into the surrounding region. Some leave their desert communities for seasonal work. Others are leaving to find work and education. Some will come back as specialists. Many will never return to their communities. After all, it is very hard to fight for survival against the inhospitable Sahara.

The Farmer and His Axe: A Greek Folktale

Retold by Robert Kang

Unknown Words

avaricious	precious	slyly
destitute	recompense	

Long ago, a destitute farmer lived in a house near the river. He had almost nothing to call his own, only this tiny house and the ancient axe he used to chop wood so he could stay warm.

One day, as he walked near the river, the axe slipped out of his hand and tumbled down the bank into the river. The man cried out in sorrow, because that axe was so precious to him.

A great fish in the river heard this cry and came to see what the trouble was. The farmer explained about the lost axe and begged the fish to help. The fish dived down and came back with an axe made entirely of gold. The farmer said this one was not his. Next, the fish brought up a silver axe, but the farmer again said this silver axe was not his. Finally, the fish brought up the familiar old axe.

"That one is mine," said the honest farmer.

"No," said the great fish, "all three are yours as a reward, for you didn't lie and claim any axe except the one that belonged to you."

The farmer accepted the axes and ran to town to tell everyone about his good fortune.

There was an avaricious shopkeeper who heard this tale and decided to try to get his own golden axe. He took his old axe to the river, threw it in, and pretended to cry about his loss. The great fish came at once and heard this man's story, and then he went and brought another golden axe. "Is this one yours?" the fish asked.

"Yes, it is," the man answered slyly, but of course, the fish knew better.

"You are not truthful," the fish said. "This is not your axe." With a splash, he disappeared under the water, and the man got neither a new axe nor his old one back, in recompense for his lie.

Reaching for the Sky

by Nathan Oberle

Unknown Words

aviation	discrimination	gifted
cargo	encourage	opportunities

Bessie Coleman was a dreamer. She was one of thirteen children. Her parents were farm workers in Texas, and most of the children joined them in the fields. Bessie was different. She was very gifted at mathematics, so her family helped her continue her education. This was unusual at the time, because in the early 1900s, African American women had few opportunities for education and careers.

Coleman moved to Chicago to work. There, she became interested in the new field of aviation, flying! She wanted to become a pilot, but she wasn't allowed in the aviation schools. So she took a big step: She learned French and moved to France, where she was accepted into a famous aviation school. She finally learned to fly airplanes and became the first American woman to have an international pilot's license.

Because of continued discrimination, Coleman could not fly airplanes with passengers or cargo. Instead, she became a stunt pilot. She had her first show in the United States in September 1922. She was a popular performer at air shows around the country. She used her popularity to challenge racism and to encourage other African Americans to become pilots. She raised money to help others learn to fly. She even dreamed of opening her own aviation school. Unfortunately, Coleman died in an accident during a practice flight when she was only thirty-three. Still, her bravery paved the way for other women and other African Americans to learn the freedom of flying.

Producing Paper

by Jacob Gilmartin

A worker removes handmade paper from a screen.

Latin Word Origins

animal	popular	producing
centuries	portable	similar
differ	process	vellum
manufacturing		

97

Suppose you want to write a quick note to a friend. All you have to do is reach into your backpack, grab your notebook, and tear out a sheet of paper. That seems simple enough. But the invention and manufacturing of inexpensive paper for everyday use wasn't that simple. Papermaking was a process that grew up over the course of many centuries.

For thousands of years, when people wanted to write or draw, their choices were limited. Of course, they could paint on cave walls and carve in stone, but that wasn't portable. People began to paint or write on animal skins. However, animal skins weren't available all the time, and they were messy to prepare. In the second century B.C., a process was developed for making parchment. This involved cleaning and scrubbing the skins and stretching them thin. They were then dried and treated to make a better writing surface. People could write on both sides of parchment. This led to the development of bound books, which soon replaced scrolls. People began to use softer, thinner skins to produce vellum, a finer parchment popular in Europe. Still, parchment and vellum were time-consuming to make and expensive to buy. They were used only for the most important writing.

Centuries earlier, the Egyptians had found many uses for the papyrus plant. One use was the making of fine writing material. The word *paper* actually comes from the name of this plant. The Egyptians could lay fibers from the papyrus plant together, dampen them with water, and press them firmly. When these fibers were dry, they were pounded into thin sheets and dried thoroughly in the sun. Papyrus was very fine and smooth, but it was more expensive than vellum.

The first paper made from pulp was made in China around A.D. 100. Pulp is a substance made of water and fine fibers. This first paper was made of mulberry plant fibers and old bits of net and rags. It was strong and inexpensive. It took centuries for this method to move west. It was being used in Central Asia and the Middle East in the 700s before arriving in Europe. The invention of printing in the 1400s increased demand for inexpensive paper. Many paper mills sprang up as a result. These mills often used cotton or linen rags to make the pulp. When these became hard to find, they began to rely on wood pulp and vegetable matter.

Around 1798 a man named Nicholas-Louis Robert invented a machine to make paper. It had moving screens that were dipped mechanically into a vat of pulp. Other improvements and inventions followed. But even 2000 years later, with all the modern technology available, paper is still made by the same basic process. A pulp is made of finely chopped fibers and water. A screen is used to make a sheet of these fibers. This sheet is pressed to squeeze out the water, then dried and pressed again. The quality of the paper may differ depending on the types of fibers. Though paper is usually made by machine now, similar principles still apply.

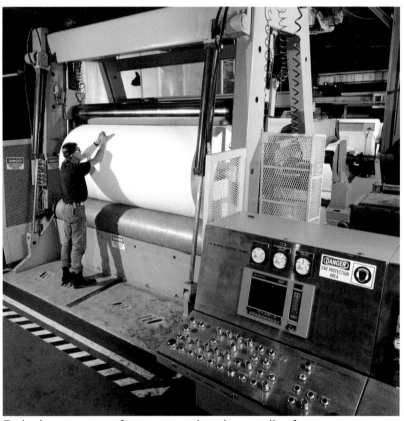

Today's paper manufacturers produce large rolls of paper.

The Long Road to Freedom

by Angela Bruner

Latin Word Origins

complete	formal	journey
constantly	fortunate	lingo
courageous	functioning	referred

The journey was hundreds of miles and could take weeks to complete. It was dangerous, and the end was uncertain. Avid slave hunters were on the lookout constantly, ready to capture runaway slaves for big rewards. Yet thousands of enslaved people risked everything to make their escape. All the fear and strain of the journey was worth it for this one chance at freedom.

Many of these runaways were fortunate to have help from a network of people dubbed the Underground Railroad. This wasn't a formal organization. There were no clear leaders or headquarters. Different people involved in fighting slavery and helping runaway slaves simply became connected through word of mouth. They were able to work together to find safe places for escaping slaves. They gathered money and supplies to help them on their way and got them jobs and homes in Canada.

The Underground Railroad wasn't really connected to the railways, but they borrowed the lingo of the railways to keep their secrets safe. "Conductors" were guides who helped move escaping slaves from the plantations in the South to various safe houses and on to Canada. These safe stops were referred to as "stations" or "depots." The hosts were called "stationmasters." "Packages" or "freight" was code for the escaping slaves.

Many of the conductors and stationmasters were former slaves themselves. They risked their own freedom to help others escape. The courageous people who kept the Underground Railroad functioning brought tens of thousands of people to freedom.

Grandma's Cuckoo Clock

by Lucy Folks

Latin Word Origins

antique	explained	organize
appeared	intently	perfectly
compensation		

Miriam could tell Grandma Doris was sad. When the movers had brought her things into the new apartment, one box had fallen. The antique cuckoo clock inside had broken into a dozen pieces. Grandma said it was all right, but she kept looking up at the wall where the clock should have been.

Grandma had once explained that the clock had belonged to her grandmother, Miriam's great-great-grandmother. She had brought the clock with her from Germany when she came to America in 1910. The clock reminded Miriam of the stories she had heard about the Old World.

Miriam wanted to do something to make her Grandma less sad, so she began looking in the windows of local antique stores. She saw lots of clocks, but none that were quite like the broken one. One day, just two weeks before Grandma's birthday, a beautiful little cuckoo clock appeared in the window of Main Street Antiques. The price tag said it cost 100 dollars. The owner saw her looking intently at the clock.

"Can I help you, young lady?" she asked kindly.

Miriam explained the problem. The owner nodded her head in understanding.

"You might be able to help me out with something," the owner said. "If you can help me organize my files, I think we could consider that clock fair compensation. What do you think?"

Miriam leaped at the chance. Every day after school, she helped with the files. Soon, they were perfectly organized. On Grandma's birthday, Miriam came home proudly with the little clock. The tears of joy in Grandma's eyes were the best reward.

Gymnastics with Giselle

by Kai Autaubo

Greek Roots

athletic	enthusiasm	gymnasts
basic	enthusiastically	parallel
choreography	gymnastics	

Giselle looked miserable. She had had the cast on for just over a week, but the cast wasn't her main problem. Her broken foot meant she couldn't compete at the upcoming gymnastics meet, for which she had been training for two months. Brianna tried to distract her, but Giselle was still sulking.

"Do you want to go to the movies or something instead?" Brianna asked.

"No, I want to go and cheer the other girls," Giselle said.

"Well, could I come with you?" Brianna asked, which caused Giselle's face to brighten.

"That would be great," she replied enthusiastically.

Saturday came, and Giselle and Brianna entered the enormous stadium and searched for Giselle's teammates. The whole team was busy stretching and warming up their muscles so they wouldn't hurt themselves. Giselle said hello and wished them all luck. Then she and Brianna found seats where they could see several different competition areas, and Giselle told Brianna some basic information about gymnastics.

"Gymnasts have to be super athletic and strong, because they do a lot of demanding activities," she said. She pointed out a gymnast on two bars that were nearby, a few feet from the ground. "Those are parallel bars. The gymnast swings, spins, and does turns and handstands on these bars while holding his feet up off the ground. His shoulders and arms have to be really strong."

Then she pointed out a wider, lower bar. "That is the balance beam. We do jumps, flips, and handstands on the beam, but we have to keep our balance or we'll fall." She frowned and pointed to the cast. "That's how I did this."

Giselle's attention was pulled away for a minute while one of her teammates did a floor routine on a large mat in the center of the stadium. She cheered when her friend finished and sighed. "That is my favorite event," she said. "The choreography can be so beautiful, and you get to move so much more freely. I've been working on doing more backflips. I can already do four in a row!"

Giselle's enthusiasm for gymnastics was infectious. Brianna tried to imagine herself running, leaping, and flipping gracefully across the floor, but she laughed a little at the picture in her head.

Giselle continued her explanation of the different events. "That thing that looks like a bench is a vaulting table," she said. "To do a vault, a gymnast runs toward the table, jumps on a springboard, and then does some flips before landing on the other side. It is really hard to do that and still land right."

Brianna was pleased to see that Giselle was so excited to be talking about gymnastics that she had stopped being grumpy. She pointed this out to her friend, who grinned. "Well, there's nothing I can do about the cast, so I might as well just relax and enjoy the day, right? Thanks for coming with me so I could share my love for gymnastics with you."

Brianna laughed and said, "I should be thanking you! You've given me such a fun glimpse of how amazing this sport can be that I might just have to give it a try myself!"

Bell's Bright Idea

by Allen Edwards

Greek Roots

electrical	logical	technology
electricity	symbols	telegraph
emphasis	systems	telephone
enthusiasm		

"Watson, come here, I want you." With those simple words, a new era began. Those are the words Alexander Graham Bell, a young inventor, spoke into the first telephone. His assistant Thomas Watson heard them loud and clear in another room of the house. In that moment, the possibilities of almost instant communication changed the world.

Bell didn't start out planning to completely change the way people communicate. His original emphasis was on helping people with hearing impairments. He thought the new discoveries about electricity might hold the key. He began working on his inventions.

Already people communicated by telegraph, sending messages as electrical impulses along wires. It seemed logical to Bell that, if the human voice could be turned into electrical impulses, it too could be carried on these wires. A receiver on the other end would then need to turn the electrical impulses back into recognizable speech. His enthusiasm for electrical technology led to four years of experiments with this concept. Finally, on March 10, 1876, Bell successfully tested his device.

It wasn't long before telephone systems connected people all over the nation and all over the world. Now telephones are in every home and almost every pocket, symbols of our great longing to be connected.

Meeting Mr. President

by Hannah McGlynn

Greek Roots

autograph	enthusiastically	philosophy
biography	idiot	politics
democracy		

It was hard to get through all the crowds at the bookstore. David couldn't imagine what had brought so many people to the store. He just wanted to find one magazine and get back home. Unfortunately, as he tried to get to the counter to pay, the crowd was thicker than ever and he couldn't go another inch. Then a voice near him began speaking loudly.

"Ladies and gentlemen, it is such an honor to have as our guest the former President of the United States to meet people and sign his new book," the lady said. David's eyes nearly popped out of his head, because right behind the woman was a face he recognized from the news. The lady continued.

"His new biography is an amazing look at one man's work to keep democracy strong," she said. "It's not about politics or philosophy. It's about standing up for what we believe in. Let's give him a warm welcome!"

The crowd clapped enthusiastically. Then they lined up to get his autograph in their books. David thought this was probably a once-in-a-lifetime chance, so he got in the long line and waited too. When he got to the table, David felt like an idiot. He didn't have a book for the man to sign! But the former president just looked at David and winked. He pulled a book from the box beside him, signed it, and handed it to David.

"What's your name, young man?" he asked.

"David, sir," David answered shyly.

"Well, David, I hope you'll read this for me and let me know what you think," the president said. "Someday it will be your turn to lead, and I'd like to know your opinion."

David shook his hand, thanked him, and promised to read it before making his way happily home.

Old Faithful

by Caleb Alvarez

Yellowstone National Park is home to colorful hot pools like this one as well as to geysers.

Related Words (Base Words with Endings)

curious/curiosity	large/largest	predict/predicting/ prediction
erupt(s)/ eruption(s)	observed/ observation	
exact/exactly		regular/regularity

The name says it all . . . sort of. Old Faithful is the most famous geyser in the world. It is also one of the largest. Geysers are holes in the ground through which hot water and gases erupt. Old Faithful got its name because of its apparent regularity. Visitors and rangers in Yellowstone National Park observed that Old Faithful would spout every 63 to 70 minutes. In truth, Old Faithful is less regular in its eruptions than was once thought. Further observation showed that the eruptions come at very different intervals. You might have to wait anywhere from 60 to 110 minutes for an eruption. A large earthquake in 1983 may have played a part in disrupting the regularity. It is impossible to predict exactly when Old Faithful will blow. However, there does seem to be a connection between the length of the eruption and how long of a wait there will be before the next one.

Old Faithful erupts for $1\frac{1}{2}$ to $5\frac{1}{2}$ minutes. It releases as much as 8,400 gallons of water each time. The water temperature is usually above 200 degrees Fahrenheit, close to boiling. A short burst means the next eruption will come sooner. The longer and more powerful eruptions seem to cause a longer wait. Eruptions are usually between 130 and 140 feet high. However, some reach as high as 180 feet. Old Faithful is one of many geysers in Yellowstone's Upper Geyser Basin. Dozens of geysers and hot springs can be found within an area of about two square miles. In fact, this little area encloses about one quarter of all the world's geysers!

Thousands of people visit Yellowstone every year. They are curious about Old Faithful and the other geysers. Geologists and seismologists are also quite interested. In 2013 their curiosity was finally rewarded. The mystery of Old Faithful's ongoing eruptions was uncovered. A widely accepted theory said that geysers come through a long natural tube. That couldn't explain the ongoing, somewhat regular eruptions. New studies suggest something different. The caverns under Old Faithful are more egg-shaped. They have pockets and branching tunnels. It appears that Old Faithful's eruptions are due to steam bubbles that get trapped in these spaces. When one of these "bubble traps" pops, pressure changes in the caverns and water explodes out. They still cannot make predictions about exact times of eruptions. Nevertheless, this new knowledge of the workings under the geyser has added to our understanding about seismic activity below the earth's surface.

In 2010 the Old Faithful Visitor Education Center opened. If you ever find yourself in the neighborhood, you can stop for a view of the world's most famous geyser. Then take time to visit the center. There you will learn about the fascinating geology and geothermal properties of the region. You can try your hand at predicting the eruptions. How close do you think you can get? Whatever you do, whatever you learn, the best part is just experiencing Old Faithful. Seeing that majestic plume of steam and water rising into the sky will be a sight to remember.

Yellowstone's Old Faithful is one of more than 300 geysers in the park.

The Chinatown Photo Hunt

by Juanita Lucas

Related Words (Base Words with Endings)

certainly/
uncertainty

culture/cultural/
culturally

different/
differently

excited/
excitement

imagination/
imaginative

photograph/
photographer

tradition/
traditional

Jared climbed off the school bus, his mom right behind him. He was excited to be on a cultural field trip in the big city, but the excitement was mixed with uncertainty. This felt somehow more foreign. Maybe it was because they were in Chinatown, seeing Chinese characters on Chinese signs. All the sights, sounds, and smells were new for him.

They had been studying traditional Chinese culture in their social studies class, and their teacher thought it would be nice to see some of the bits and pieces of that culture that still survive in the American heartland. Today they had an assignment. They were given a list of different things to look for and photograph. Jared was no photographer, but he was eager to see what he could capture. As they walked around Chinatown, the students were encouraged to look around for the items.

This wasn't a boring list, asking for simple things like "Chinese food" or "fish." The list was full of interesting and challenging things. For example, he had to find a mural that showed one principle of Confucianism. He had to find an example of a Buddhist tradition. He had to learn and then locate the written Chinese character for luck. He had to have a picture of himself with a thousand-year-old egg. The list was very imaginative, so Jared was forced to use his imagination too. It certainly helped him to see this culturally rich community differently than if he'd just come down with his parents for a quick bite to eat.

Wild About Water Balloons

by Adam Engelking

Related Words (Base Words with Endings)

creating/ creation/ creative/ creativity

eager/eagerly

imagination / imagined

invent/ inventing/ invention/ inventors

modifications/ modify

spray/sprayer

support/ supportive

Lexi Glenn had a problem. She liked to have water-balloon tosses with her friends, but filling the balloons was a hassle. If she did it in the bathroom, she inevitably got water all over the floor and herself. If she did it with a hose outside, she ended up wasting lots of water and creating a little lake around her. How could she get past this problem?

Lexi, who was eight years old at the time, decided to get creative. She remembered seeing a garden spray bottle in the garage. She imagined how she could fill a balloon in a more controlled way with the sprayer. Eager to test her idea, she dug out the sprayer. After washing it well, she filled it with water and gave it a try. It worked! She ran inside to show off her new invention. Lexi made a few modifications to the bottle to get it just right.

Lexi thought about how to share her invention with more kids. In her imagination, she could see herself starting a business to make and sell her creation. She continued to modify the design to get her water-balloon filler ready to sell. Then, with the support of her family and friends, she went into business. Soon, Lexi's invention was on the shelves of hundreds of toy stores. Customers have loved the balloon filler and eagerly bought them.

Lexi has continued to invent other products, letting her own creativity and curiosity guide her. Her supportive family has stood beside her through all the challenges of running a business. Lexi also wrote a book about her inventing. She wants to encourage other children to use their creativity to become inventors. This creative young woman is an inspiration to many kids.

The Play's the Thing . . .

by Jessica Fehrman

Latin Roots *struct, scrib, script*

construction	description	instructor
describing	instructions	script

Nick had been chosen for the lead in the school play. He had loved every minute of it. It gave him the acting bug, his dad had said. Nick was looking forward to the spring play.

Mr. Macomber, the drama instructor, knew about Nick's interest. One day he saw an announcement from a nearby college for a young playwrights competition. The instructions said submissions should be one-act plays written by students. Nick wrote stories for the school newsletter that were quite good. Maybe this would be a good way to combine Nick's writing skills with his growing love of theater. Mr. Macomber handed Nick the description of the competition when he saw him the next day.

Nick got to work right away on a script. He had loads of ideas in his head, but getting them on paper was hard work. He realized that a script must do without all the describing words that you use in stories to draw the reader in. Instead, a playwright has to rely on dialogue and stage directions to make sure the story comes out well.

By the next week, Nick had his play written and ready to submit. Mr. Macomber read it and smiled, believing that Nick would have a really good chance of winning.

Weeks passed without any news. In February, Mr. Macomber announced the tryouts for the spring play, and Nick was so excited. However, a letter arrived the day before tryouts that changed everything. Nick's play was one of three that were chosen to be performed in the college's one-act play festival, and they wanted Nick to be a junior director. That would take a lot of time, and it meant he wouldn't have time to be in the school play. Mr. Macomber could see that Nick was torn, but he didn't pressure him either way. Nick decided he would work with the college to stage his play.

Every afternoon, while his drama club friends went to practice for the school play, Nick biked over to the college campus to work with the festival director. Kristy had lots of good ideas, but she wanted Nick to be part of the planning too. He learned about lighting and scenery construction. He learned about costume design and sound setups. Then rehearsals began, and Nick was in awe. The actors who were playing his characters made them come alive in ways he had hardly imagined. It was absolutely amazing to see his imagination becoming reality on a stage. As the weekend of the festival drew near, Nick forgot about his disappointment over the school play. Mr. Macomber came to the play along with Nick's family, and they clapped enthusiastically with the whole audience when it was over. It was done so quickly, after all those weeks of preparation! Nick felt a little disappointed again.

The following weekend was the school play. Nick felt odd being a part of the audience instead of on stage. When the play ended and the curtain had closed, Mr. Macomber came on stage and asked the audience to stay seated.

"Tonight, ladies and gentlemen, you will get two shows for the price of one," he said. "Our students have prepared another short play for you. We hope you enjoy it."

The curtain rose on a different set. When the first line was spoken, Nick realized this was his play, being performed by his friends, in his school. It was even better than the festival performance. Nick could not remember ever being happier.

Don't Just Recycle . . . Upcycle!

by Joy Hershey

> **Latin Roots** *struct, scrib, script*
>
> | | | |
> |---|---|---|
> | construct | descriptions | instructions |
> | describe | indestructible | subscribe |

We have all heard the three Rs for being responsible for the environment: reduce, reuse, recycle. But some people are getting really creative with their environmental awareness and taking it to a whole new level.

"Upcycling" or "supercycling" are new phrases. They describe the process of turning something that used to be garbage into something new and wonderful. Old things are getting a very stylish new life. Do you have a bunch of plastic water bottles waiting to go to recycling? Why not turn them into a cute bowling game for a younger sibling? And how about those piles and piles of plastic bags? With a little effort and creativity, they can be turned into pretty baskets, jewelry, even shoes and belts, all of them practically indestructible. Old vinyl records (your grandparents might still have some somewhere) can be used as table decorations or molded into different shapes. Ugly old neckties your dad is too embarrassed to wear can become super-chic bags. You can construct a great desk out of old stools and a door. The possibilities are truly endless!

You can find websites with all sorts of pictures, descriptions, and instructions online. There are also specialty blogs and upcycling newsletters you can subscribe to. (Remember to get your parents' permission first!) Keep your eyes open for things that might still have life in them. Then give upcycling a try. You may find that being environmentally responsible has never been so much fun.

Following the Doctor's Orders

by Billy Quintana

Latin Roots *struct, scrib, script*

constructive	prescribed	scribbled
instructions	prescription	

It had been raining every day since we left for vacation. My sister Emma and I had been going a little crazy, being stuck inside. This particular morning had started with a quarrel about who had lost my shoes. That had turned into an argument about who could have the last of the cereal. The bickering had lasted until nearly lunch time. Dad was trying to read a book on the covered front porch. He finally gave up and called us outside.

"Now look, girls, this quarreling has to stop," he said firmly. I started to complain, but he held up a hand to stop me.

"I know I'm on vacation, but I'm going to become Dr. Dad for a moment and write you a prescription," he said, pulling out the pad of paper he used at the office. He scribbled something, tore off the sheet, and handed it to me. In big letters, he had written, "Do something constructive." We were both a little puzzled as we went back inside.

"What does he mean, that we should build a building or something?" Emma asked.

"No, I think it means to do something positive instead of arguing with each other," I said.

"Let's go ask Mom if she has something constructive we can do," Emma suggested.

Mom, of course, had wisely packed all sorts of things to do. We chose a craft kit for making sand art. We worked together to follow the instructions. Pretty soon, the whole afternoon had passed without a single quarrel or complaint. The advice Dad had prescribed had cured our stuck-inside blues.

The Need for Speed

by Melissa Wallace

Related Words

big/bigger	fast/faster/fastest	muscles/muscular
compare/comparison	flight/flightless	speed/speedsters/speedy
considering/consideration	impressed/impressive	

Everyone is in a hurry sometimes. Maybe when you are about to miss the bus, you start moving pretty fast. Maybe you can really put the speed on when your brother challenges you to a race but gets a head start. But even the fastest humans move like snails in comparison to some animals. In the animal world, speed can make the difference between life and death. It can mean having enough food or starving.

The fastest animal on the planet is the peregrine falcon. These strong, swift birds have a regular flight rate of about 90 miles per hour. That is faster than the legal speed limit for cars anywhere in the United States.

Peregrine falcons tend to make their nests in high places, such as the tops of cliffs or even skyscrapers. They then catch their prey by diving at them out of the sky. During these dives, a falcon can reach a speed of more than 200 miles per hour. Most cars aren't designed to go even close to that speed! The falcon uses this incredible speed to kill its prey on impact. These amazing birds can be found all over the world. In recent decades they have been endangered in some places, including the United States.

Animals in the feline family can really put on the speed, too. The cheetah is the fastest land animal. This sleek, graceful cat can reach 70 miles an hour when chasing its prey. That's almost three times faster than the fastest human runner! A cheetah's body is designed for sprinting. It has a long body and long, thin legs that give it bigger strides than most big cats. Its muscles and internal organs are really efficient too. This gives a cheetah the energy it needs for high-speed sprints. This sleek animal lives mostly in Africa, though at one time it was common in Asia as well. In the past, cheetahs were sometimes tamed and used by hunters to capture prey. They also were kept as pets by royalty.

The fastest animal in the ocean would have almost no problem keeping up with the speedy cheetah. The sailfish can swim at speeds of nearly 70 miles an hour. The sailfish got its name because of its enormous dorsal fin (*dorsal* means "back"). The fin stretches nearly the whole length of its long, muscular body. It is really tall, so that it resembles a sail on a boat. Sailfish live in the warmer parts of the Atlantic, Pacific, and Indian Oceans.

Some other animals hit impressive speeds, too, considering the size of their bodies. A tiger beetle can go about 5.6 miles an hour. That may not sound like much. But take into consideration how small those insect legs are. Tiger beetles are only about a half-inch long. Their top speed is equivalent to a human being running 480 miles per hour. That's fast!

Ostriches also deserve honorable mention. These funny, flightless birds, with their long necks and legs, are the largest living birds. They can reach speeds of about 45 miles an hour, making them the fastest birds on land.

The fastest dog can run almost 40 miles an hour. With their long, graceful legs and bodies, greyhounds were bred for hunting and racing. Now, these gentle, intelligent animals are becoming more popular as show dogs and companions.

Compare these amazing speedsters to human speed records. Jamaican runner Usain Bolt set a world-record speed of about 28 miles an hour. That's not cheetah speed, but it is incredible nonetheless. Bolt's record impressed the whole world. Other runners are aiming to reach the limits of human speed too.

Lights, Camera, Action!

by Greg Malick

Related Words

brief/briefly

directed/director

excited/exciting/excitement

participate/participation

permit/permission

real/really/unreal

speech/speechless

transformed/transformation

The whole town was buzzing with the news that a real Hollywood movie was being filmed right here in their hometown. Overnight, trailers and trucks arrived with filming equipment and filmmaking professionals. The downtown area was transformed into a movie set. This was an exciting experience for their small town!

Jacob and Ben rode their bikes to where all the excitement was, hoping to catch a glimpse of some famous movie stars. They never expected to become movie stars themselves, but the movie's director saw them sitting on the curb, watching wide-eyed. He asked them if they'd like to be in the movie, which left the boys speechless. They raced home with permission slips that their mother needed to sign. She agreed to permit them to participate, but only on the condition that she meet the director first.

The next day the boys went back to the set with their mom. She talked briefly with the director about the boys' participation. Then she signed the form and left them to their work. "Have fun!" she called after them as they were directed to the makeup trailer.

Jacob and Ben were on the set all day that Saturday. The scene they were to be in was brief, and they each only had one line of speech, but they were still excited to be there. They did meet some movie stars, but even more fun was talking to the camera operators and the other professionals about their work. They never knew it took so many people to make a movie!

By the next weekend, the trailers and trucks were all gone and the transformation back to a quiet little town was complete. The whole experience seemed a little unreal, like a dream. The boys had to wait months until the movie was released to see proof that they had really been in a movie.

The Longest Walk

by Karis Melito

Related Words

beauty/beautiful

challenge/
challenging

dangers/
dangerous

exhausted/
exhaustion

hike/hikers/
hiking

inspired/
inspiration

possibility/
impossible

weak/weaker/
weakness

Martin sat down on a large rock and wiped his forehead. He looked at the beautiful mountain view around him. It was hard to believe that he was so close to reaching his goal. After many years, he was about to finish walking the 2,700-mile Pacific Crest Trail.

The Pacific Crest Trail was beautiful, but it was dangerous as well. Weather could change quickly and become harsh, and rockslides and wild animals were real dangers too. Martin had an extra challenge to deal with.

It was amazing that Martin could walk at all, because he had been born with a disease that made the muscles in his legs and feet very weak. He had had three operations as a child and used a wheelchair for a while. But Martin was born in the shadow of the Sierra Nevada mountains, and he was inspired by the beauty he saw. He worked hard to overcome the weakness in his legs. He began taking short hikes. He got a job in the national park so he could keep hiking.

Martin dreamed of hiking the whole Pacific Crest Trail. Many would have said this was impossible. Even strong hikers found this trail challenging. It was easy to become exhausted on the steep paths. But Martin decided the time had come to turn this impossible dream into a possibility.

Martin started hiking the trail in segments, for a week or two at a time. Sometimes his wife or sons would hike with him, and other times he would invite friends. His best hiking pal was his brother Pat. Over the years, the disease started to take its toll. His legs were getting weaker, and he fought exhaustion and pain. But he kept going.

Now he had one segment left to go. With a pack on his back and Pat at his side, Martin set off to reach his goal. After 15 years of walking these paths, Martin finally finished. Along the way, he became an inspiration to many people.

Let Freedom Ring

by Katy Lynch

The Liberty Bell in Philadelphia, Pennsylvania, is a symbol of American freedom.

Multiple-Meaning Words

cause	myth	still
date	ordered	well
land	ring	

The Liberty Bell is housed across the street from Independence Hall in the Liberty Bell Center. It has been a symbol of freedom for more than two centuries. The first bell in the Pennsylvania State House (later renamed Independence Hall) was made in London, England. The Pennsylvania colonial government had ordered the bell in honor of the fiftieth anniversary of the colony's Charter of Privileges. This document named some of the rights and liberties the colonists enjoyed.

The bell cracked soon after it arrived and couldn't be used. The leaders of Pennsylvania ordered a new bell to be made from the metal of that first bell. They ordered the following words to be carved on the bell: "Proclaim LIBERTY throughout all the Land unto all the inhabitants thereof." This time local metal workers cast the new bell. The bell makers also added their names and the date the bell was made. In 1753, the State House bell was hung in the tower. It was rung to announce important events.

The Liberty Bell is impressive in size. It weighs over 2,000 pounds, and its clapper weighs almost 50 pounds. The bell is almost 3 feet high and has a circumference of 12 feet at its lip. It hangs from a heavy wooden yoke.

Legend says that the bell was rung in July 1776 to announce the completion of the Declaration of Independence. Experts point out that this is probably a myth. The bell tower was in such bad condition that it would have been hard to ring the bell. Still, the legend lives on.

The name "Liberty Bell" didn't come into use until the 1830s. Abolitionists, people who worked to end slavery, used the bell as a symbol for their cause. The words on the bell seemed to apply especially well to the fight to end slavery. A poem published in 1839 in an abolitionist pamphlet was the first time the name appeared in print. The name stuck, and the Pennsylvania State House bell has been called the Liberty Bell ever since.

The bell was cracked and repaired several times. Finally in 1846 it cracked beyond repair and was never rung again. In the late 1800s, the bell toured the nation. It was displayed in Atlanta, Boston, Chicago, and San Francisco. It made stops in other places too. This enabled Americans throughout the nation to see this symbol of freedom. Its last trip was in 1915 and then it returned home to Philadelphia, where it has remained ever since. Still, the Liberty Bell has been preserved as a symbol of freedom. Today the bell has a place of honor in Liberty Bell Center.

There on every Fourth of July, children tap the bell thirteen times. The children who tap the bell are descended from the signers of the Declaration of Independence. The bell tapping honors the fifty-six signers of the Declaration. It also honors the many patriots from the thirteen colonies who worked to gain freedom from Britain.

Supreme Court Justice Samuel Alito and Mayor John Street of Philadelphia watch three young boys tap the Liberty Bell on July 4, 2006.

Biking for a Cause

by Keith Benevidez

Multiple-Meaning Words

cause	drew	right
class	host	set
date	left	spoke

While Ms. Stine's class was completing a unit on current events, they read about a recent earthquake and the terrible damage it had caused. It had left tens of thousands of people homeless. The class had a big discussion about how they could help the people there.

The students agreed to work together to support an organization that was working in the disaster area. Because it was such an important cause, the students got busy right away, generating ideas about what they could do.

Students made a number of suggestions for how to participate, and then they voted. The idea that received the most votes was a suggestion to host a bike-a-thon. Students spoke with the owners of local businesses to get their support for the event. They worked with local officials to set a date, plan a route, and organize other details, and then they posted flyers to invite people from the community to participate. Some businesses donated snacks and prizes for the bikers. Excitement about the event grew as the big day drew near.

Finally the day of the bike-a-thon came. Ms. Stine's students along with many others from their school showed up with their bikes decorated with balloons and streamers. They biked around town, with family and friends cheering them on along the route. When the day was over, more than $3,000 had been raised to help the people who had been affected by the earthquake. The students were proud of their accomplishment.

Missing Pieces

by Margaret Wu

Multiple-Meaning Words

down	lay	right
groom	left	rose
hit	pride	well
last		

Dana was really good at putting together puzzles. For her birthday, someone gave her a puzzle with a thousand pieces. It was the biggest puzzle she had ever worked on. It was going well and she was about halfway done when disaster struck. Without warning, her big tabby cat, Babe, leaped on the table, slid on the slick surface, and hit the puzzle. Pieces scattered left and right. Babe lay down lazily where the puzzle had been to groom his fur.

Dana leaped up and pointed at the scattered pieces. "Look what you did, you crazy cat!" she said angrily. Babe opened his eyes a bit, but was unmoved. She knew very well that yelling wouldn't help. Dana got on her hands and knees and began gathering the pieces. She rose at last, gave one more angry look at the cat, and went to her room to start over.

When she got close to the end, Dana realized she didn't have all of the pieces to the puzzle. There were holes here and there that she couldn't fill. She went back to the family room, where the puzzle had gone flying and searched high and low for the missing pieces. Finally, in a flowerpot on the windowsill she found the last two pieces. With pride, Dana returned to her room and put the final pieces in place. Her first thousand-piece puzzle lay complete in front of her. It was a huge picture of a sleeping tabby cat that looked just like Babe.

Acknowledgments

Photographs:

2 ©Universal Images Group Limited/Alamy; **4** ©North Wind Picture Archives/Alamy; **10** ©Everett Collection Inc/Alamy; **12** ©Image Asset Management Ltd./Alamy; **19** MARCO DE SWART/EPA/Newscom; **25** Marcio Jose Bastos Silva/Shutterstock; **28** Louie and Deneve Bunde/Photolibrary/Getty Images; **33** ©D. Hurst/Alamy; **35** Cristian Lazzari/E+/Getty Images; **41** jccommerce/Vetta/Getty Images; **43** Stewart Cohen/Blend Images/Getty Images; **49** ©Michael Snell/Alamy; **51** Crater of Diamonds State Park/AP Photo; **58** Obregon, Jose Maria (1832–1902)/Museo Nacional de Arte, Mexico/The Bridgeman Art Library; **59** ©H. Mark Weidman Photography/Alamy; **66** ©Tim Ridley/Dorling Kindersley; **68** Peter Stanley/Getty Images; **73** Scott Olson/Getty Images; **75** ©PinkShot/Fotolia; **81** American School, (19th century)/Private Collection/Peter Newark American Pictures/The Bridgeman Art Library; **82** ©Karina Baumgart/Fotolia; **89** ©Travel/Alamy; **97** Tao Xiyi/ZUMAPRESS/Newscom; **100** ©H. Mark Weidman Photography/Alamy; **105** BananaStock/Thinkstock; **108** Julie Toy/Riser/Getty Images; **113** Krzysztof Wiktor/Shutterstock; **116** ©Silvy K/Fotolia; **121** ©Pearson Education, Inc.; **124** ©Pearson Education, Inc.; **129** ©blickwinkel/Alamy; **130** ©Arco Images GmbH/Alamy; **137** Mark Krapels/Shutterstock; **140** Mark Stehle/AP Photo.

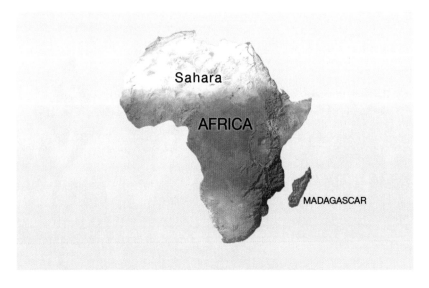